36 Great U.S. Mountain Retirement Towns

Written and Edited by Kris Kelley

D1527588

Published by Webwerxx, Inc. © 2021

Notes:

Numerous efforts have been made to verify the accuracy of the information in this report, but some information, particularly home prices, may have changed since publication. As a result, the accuracy of the content contained within this book is not guaranteed. Please conduct your own due diligence before choosing a retirement town.

Cover Photo by Simon Berger

ISBN: 9798766347606

Table of Contents

Introduction 5

Flagstaff, Arizona 7

Payson, Arizona 9

Prescott, Arizona 11

Show Low, Arizona...........................13

Mountain Home, Arkansas 15

Russellville, Arkansas 17

Breckenridge, Colorado......................19

Dolores, Colorado 21

Glenwood Springs, Colorado 23

Grand Junction, Colorado 25

Manitou Springs, Colorado...................28

Blue Ridge, Georgia.........................30

Dahlonega, Georgia 31

Hiawassee, Georgia..........................33

Coeur d'Alene, Idaho........................35

Sandpoint, Idaho 38

Bozeman, Montana 40

Missoula, Montana 41

Ruidoso, New Mexico.........................44

Asheville, North Carolina...................46

Banner Elk, North Carolina..................48

Columbus, North Carolina 50

Fletcher, North Carolina 51

Lake Lure, North Carolina 53

Ashland, Oregon 54

Jacksonville, Oregon...57

Eagles Mere, Pennsylvania.....................................59

Jim Thorpe, Pennsylvania 61

Gatlinburg, Tennessee...63

Sewanee, Tennessee...65

Signal Mountain, Tennessee....................................67

Stowe, Vermont...69

Abingdon, Virginia 71

Blacksburg, Virginia...73

Morgantown, West Virginia 74

Cody, Wyoming..76

Introduction

From the Appalachians in northern Georgia to the Rockies in Montana, mountain towns across the United States beckon with their scenic surroundings, amazing views, plentiful outdoor recreation and abundant fresh air.

Not all mountain towns are created equal, though. Some have a declining population. Others have high crime statistics, poor infrastructure or a high poverty rate.

Here, however, are 36 mountain towns worth consideration when retirement time arrives. These places come in a wide price range, although livable mountain towns tend to be on the more expensive side.

All of these communities have safe neighborhoods, a local hospital or one nearby, a steady or growing population and an overall quality of life that makes them a place people want to live.

We provide an overview of each town, taking a look at population numbers, housing prices, climate, political leanings, percentage of the population age 45 or better, amenities and things to do, public transit, education levels, elevation and more.

To us, a mountain town might not have a terribly high elevation – for example, towns in the Blue Ridge Mountains do not have the same elevation as many Rocky Mountain towns – but if the town is surrounded by hills and peaks, then it is a mountain town. Similarly, if a town has a high elevation and is close to a mountain range, but not actually in the mountain range per se, then it is a mountain town.

Please note that this book is not intended to be an in-depth examination of each town. It is instead an overview, a starting point for finding the best mountain community for your retirement.

Flagstaff, Arizona

Flagstaff came into being in 1882 after a U.S. military lieutenant first scouted this area in north central Arizona for a new road and cut down a Ponderosa pine tree to use as a flag staff. The transcontinental railroad soon arrived, and for years Flagstaff thrived as a timber and cattle hub. It was later a stop on famed Route 66.

Today this mountain metropolis retains much of its Old West character and is a touristy, friendly place, surrounded by forests, mountains and desert. It also home to Northern Arizona University.

Almost everyone who comes to Flagstaff seems to enjoy it, whether it be the inspiring natural beauty, lively cultural scene or recreation opportunities. Outdoor activities, everything from hiking in the nearby canyons and kayaking on the Colorado River to alpine skiing in the San Francisco Peaks, are a way of life.

Several national parks, including the Grand Canyon National Park, are within a two-hour drive. The city has 700 acres of parks, six private and public golf courses and an extensive network of bicycle and walking trails.

Locals also enjoy a symphony orchestra and several theatre groups, including the Theatrikos Theatre Company. Northern Arizona University's award-winning theatre department mounts several

productions a year. Residents also attend opera performances, produced by the Flagstaff Light Opera

Company, as well as the works of at least three dance companies.

The downtown boasts brick sidewalks and refurbished historic structures that house a variety of retailers, shops, restaurants and galleries.

The 200-acre Arboretum at Flagstaff sits in a national forest and has 2,500 species of plants. The city is also home to two observatories and intentionally maintains dark nighttime skies. The stars, glimmering like shiny diamonds, often seem close enough to touch.

Population: 78,000 (city proper)

Age 45 or Better: 23%

Median Home Price: $555,000

Climate: Summers are cool with temperatures in the 70s and 80s, and evenings can get very chilly. Monsoon rains come in July and August. Winter temperatures are in the teens, 20s, 30s and low 40s. From November through April, the city receives an average of 95 inches of snow each year, making Flagstaff one of the nation's snowiest towns.

Elevation: 6,910 feet above sea level

Public Transit: Yes

At Least One Hospital Accepts Medicare Patients: Yes

At Least One Hospital Accredited by Joint Commission: Yes

Crime Rate: Meets the national average

Public Library: Yes

Political Leanings: Liberal

College Educated: 45%

Is Arizona Considered Tax Friendly for Retirement: Yes

Drawbacks: Wages are low, and prices are often inflated thanks to the large tourist numbers. Some people say that Flagstaff has a transitory feeling.

Notes: The city has a large student population.

Payson, Arizona

Payson is a quiet town surrounded by the sprawling Tonto National Forest at 5,000 feet above sea level in north central Arizona. It sits between Phoenix and the Mogollon Rim, a long stretch of rugged cliffs loved by outdoor adventurers. The town is accessible by two state highways.

Started as a post office in 1882, Payson was for many years just a place to stop for gas, lunch or outdoor gear before heading into the Tonto National Forest backcountry to do some fishing, boating, hiking, Jeeping or camping. Over the last 20 years, though, more folks have moved in and new homes have popped up. Many are nestled in the forest, and some are found in a fly-in neighborhood next to the airport.

The old Main Street has shops, gas stations, hardware stores, restaurants, motels and the like. Payson plays up its Western heritage for tourists and has rodeos, a fiddle contest, a Pony Express reenactment, a mud run, a summer concert series and much more.

Residents enjoy two private golf courses and some pretty parks (Green Valley Park has a lake). The Mazatzal Hotel and Casino is on the Tonto Apache Reservation outside of town and has gambling, dining and live entertainment.

Population: 16,000 (city proper)

Age 45 or Better: 62%

Median Home Price: $360,000

Climate: Summer temperatures are in the 70s, 80s and low-90s. Winter temperatures are in the 20s, 30s and 40s. On average, the area receives approximately 20 inches of rain and 20 inches of snow each year.

Elevation: 5,003 feet above sea level

Public Transit: No

At Least One Hospital Accepts Medicare Patients: Yes

At Least One Hospital Accredited by Joint Commission: Yes

Crime Rate: Meets the national average

Public Library: Yes

Political Leanings: Conservative

College Educated: 27%

Is Arizona Considered Tax Friendly for Retirement: Yes

Drawbacks: The roads in and out of town are often congested in summer and sometimes closed in winter. This area can feel a little lonely from October to April.

Notes: Payson is sometimes described as "mountain redneck." The water supply is dependent on an aquifer that is drought sensitive, so water restrictions are usually in place. Many residents live in Payson part-time.

Prescott, Arizona

At 5,400 feet above sea level in central Arizona's Bradshaw Mountains, Prescott got its start as a rowdy, hardscrabble mining camp in the early-1800s and in 1864 was named the territorial capital of Arizona. It has held onto its frontier heritage, giving it an Old West flavor that is alive and well today. It is a popular vacation and "snowbird" destination.

In its early days, Prescott brimmed with elegant architecture, including Greek Revival, Octagon and Queen Anne building styles, as lavish homes were built by miners who had become overnight millionaires. Today, more than 800 commercial buildings and residences are listed on the National Register of Historic Places.

The centerpiece of Prescott's fun downtown is Courthouse Plaza, a green, touristy oasis under the shade of giant elms. Museums, restaurants, antique stores, the 1905 Elks Opera House and historic accommodations, including the 1927 Hassayampa Inn, surround the Plaza.

Nearby Whiskey Row, an early-day saloon neighborhood and a survivor of a 1900 fire, is today a fashionable block with boutiques, cafes and galleries. The Palace Restaurant and Saloon is Arizona's oldest bar and eatery, with wooden floors, a tin ceiling and the original quarter sawn oak and cherry bar.

Festivals and events include the World's Oldest Rodeo (started in 1888), the Arizona Shakespeare Festival, the Cowboy Poets Gathering and the Prescott Bluegrass Festival.

Locals enjoy six golf courses, and Prescott National Forest is right next door with more than 450 miles of hiking, biking and horseback riding trails. Five nearby lakes provide for an abundance of fishing and boating. The back road trip up to the ghost town of Crown King is a great way to spend a Sunday afternoon, as is touring Prescott's handful of up-and-coming wineries.

Population: 44,000 (city proper)

Age 45 or Better: 55%

Median Home Price: $535,000

Climate: Summer temperatures reach into the 90s but cool off into the 50s at night. Winters are mild with temperatures in the 40s and 50s, but nights can get chilly, with temperatures dipping into the 20s. On average, the area receives 19 inches of rain and 24 inches of snow each year.

Elevation: 5,367 feet above sea level

Public Transit: Yes

At Least One Hospital Accepts Medicare Patients: Yes

At Least One Hospital Accredited by Joint Commission: No

Crime Rate: Meets the national average

Public Library: Yes

Political Leanings: Conservative

College Educated: 35%

Is Arizona Considered Tax Friendly for Retirement: Yes

Drawbacks: Traffic congestion is an issue, particularly on winter weekends when out-of-state tourists come to visit and on summer weekends when Arizona residents from hotter cities come to cool off. Water is always a concern in this part of the country, and water restrictions are often in place.

Notes: In some ways, with its mountain setting and mining history, Prescott feels as if it is in Colorado or Utah rather than in Arizona.

Show Low, Arizona

Show Low sits in northeastern Arizona's White Mountains, about three hours northeast of Phoenix, and it is tucked into a massive stand of ponderosa pines. In 1876, a young Virginian named Cooley arrived and won a poker game. His prize was the ranch that eventually became the mellow town of Show Low.

Deuce of Clubs, a reference to Show Low's beginnings, is the four lane, main drag through town. It is lined with national retailers (CSV Pharmacy, etc.), motels, strip malls, gas stations, banks, grocery stores and the like. Large box stores are along another major road to the south of town.

The White Mountain campus of Northland Pioneer College is based here and offers an array of non-credit classes for lifelong learners. The Arts Alliance of the White Mountains has a gallery and gift shop. Other local arts organizations include the Lakeside Writers Group and the White Mountain Regional Theater.

Neighborhoods are wooded and low density with manufactured homes, cabins, ranch ramblers, ranch houses, chalets and more. Many homes are vacation properties owned by Phoenix residents.

Fool Hollow Lake and Show Low Lake are popular with anglers and picnickers. Pintall Lake attracts waterfowl and bird watchers. There are 180 miles of trails within the White Mountain system, and Sunrise Peak Ski Area is only an hour away.

Population: 11,500 (city proper)

Age 45 or Better: 45%

Median Home Price: $295,000

Climate: Summer temperatures are in the 70s, 80s and 90s, and winter temperatures are in the 20s and 30s. On average, the area receives 17 inches of rain and 26 inches of snow per year.

Elevation: 6,345 feet above sea level

At Least One Hospital Accepts Medicare Patients: Yes

At Least One Hospital Accredited by Joint Commission: No. Whiteriver, about 30 miles away, has the closest accredited hospital.

Public Transit: Yes

Crime Rate: Slightly above the national average

Public Library: Yes

Political Leanings: Conservative

College Educated: 20%

Is Arizona Considered Tax Friendly for Retirement: Yes

Drawbacks: None

Notes: The town is isolated but continues to grow.

Mountain Home, Arkansas

Nestled in the rolling hills of north central Arkansas' scenic southern Ozark Mountains, rural Mountain Home is a peaceful town popular with retirees seeking a recreation oasis. Thanks to two nearby large lakes, Lake Norfork and Bull Shoals Lake, Mountain Home offers outstanding water playgrounds.

Both Lake Norfork (550 miles of shoreline), 15 minutes east of Mountain Home, and Bull Shoals Lake (1,000 miles of shoreline), 20 minutes to the west, are clean and blue. This area has been recognized as one of the top fishing spots in the country, with trout, bass, stripers, crappie and catfish in abundance. The lakes are also popular with SCUBA divers because the water is always 45 degrees or above.

On summer weekends, the lakes take on a party atmosphere. Several full-service marinas offer a wide range of recreation equipment and services, including boats rentals and sales, slip rentals and fishing guides. Some marinas have campgrounds and all have public boat launch ramps.

For people who would rather stay dry, acres and acres of public lands and wildlife management areas are open for camping, hiking and picnicking. Mountain bikers and day hikers enjoy miles of stacked loop trails that lead through several different eco systems, including both hardwood and pine forests.

Mountain Home has a bit of culture, too. The Mountain Home Symphony performs regularly, and the Twin Lakes Playhouse has a full schedule. Arkansas State University is here and presents lectures, concerts and more.

Mountain Home shopping is adequate for necessities, but high-end stores are not the norm. Dining options include fast food chains, pizza places and family-style restaurants.

Population: 14,000 (city proper)

Age 45 or Better: 58%

Median Home Price: $160,000

Climate: Summer temperatures are the 80s and 90s with plenty of humidity. Winter highs are in the 40s and 50s with lows in the 20s and 30s. The area receives roughly 45 inches of rain and eight inches of snow per year.

Elevation: 820 feet above sea level

At Least One Hospital Accepts Medicare Patients: Yes

At Least One Hospital Accredited by Joint Commission: No, Baxter Regional Medical Center is award-winning for vascular surgery.

Public Transit: Yes, a van service

Crime Rate: Meets the national average

Public Library: Yes

College Educated: 20%

Is Arkansas Considered Tax Friendly for Retirement? Yes

Drawbacks: The tornado risk is 145% above the national average.

Notes: Mountain Home is fairly isolated.

Russellville, Arkansas

Tucked away in the lush landscape of west central Arkansas, Russellville sits along the Arkansas River between the Ozark Mountains and the Ouachita Mountains. It is an unpretentious, amiable place and is home to nearly a dozen Fortune 500 companies.

The idyllic Arkansas River Valley where Russellville sits is gaining a reputation as a recreation oasis, making it difficult for even the most ardent homebody to stay inside. Neighboring 35,000-acre Lake Dardanelle, part of the river, and Lake Dardanelle State Park provide plenty of areas for camping, hiking, canoeing, rock climbing and boating.

Russellville may be best known, though, for its bass fishing. Fishing tournaments are big business, attracting anglers from around the region. Bicycling is also popular, with some of the top bicycling trails in Arkansas in and around town.

The downtown is small, authentic and populated with locally owned clothiers, banks and restaurants. The River Valley Arts Center promotes the arts through exhibits, classes and workshops. Its Art Walk is held every first Friday and gives everyone the chance to enjoy live music, great food and art displays.

Russellville is also the site of Arkansas Tech University, a four-year public institution with a good menu of athletic competitions, concerts and plays.Perhaps the biggest event is the Pope County Fair, an event full of music, livestock auctions, great food and carnival rides

Country Cupboard has organic foods, and a community farmers' market happens three days a week. There is also a farm co-op. For more in-depth shopping, Fort Smith is 75 miles away and Little Rock is 65 miles away.

Population: 30,000 (city proper)

Age 45 or Better: 33%

Median Home Price: $155,000

Climate: Summers are humid with temperatures into the 90s. Winter temperatures are in the 20s and 30s. On average, the area receives 49 inches of rain and three inches of snow per year.

Elevation: 346 feet above sea level

At Least One Hospital Accepts Medicare Patients: Yes

At Least One Hospital Accredited by Joint Commission: Yes

Public Transit: No

Crime Rate: Slightly above the national average

Public Library: Yes

College Educated: 25%

Is Arkansas Considered Tax Friendly for Retirement? Yes

Drawbacks: The tornado risk is 165% above the national average.

Notes: Arkansas Nuclear One, Arkansas' only nuclear power plant, is seven miles to the west of Russellville.

Breckenridge, Colorado

Beautiful Breckenridge, known as Breck by the locals, started out in the 1850s as a support town for gold miners in nearby Idaho Springs. It sits at 9,600 feet above sea level in spectacular northwestern Colorado and today it is the home of Breckenridge Ski Resort, the second most popular downhill ski resort in the country.

Swaddled by mountain peaks and national forest, Breckenridge is cute, trendy and touristy. The main street is full of ice cream shops, outdoor gear stores, clothing boutiques and funky bistros. The Blue River, which is actually a creek, runs through town and has a pretty park and attractive public space next to it.

Outdoor recreation could not be better. Nearly two million skiers, snowboarders and snowshoers come each year to enjoy four mountains and some of the nation's best powder. In the summer, tourists flock to town for the scenic camping spots, rugged hiking trails, quiet fly-fishing venues and miles of challenging biking paths.

Breckenridge has lots of festivals, fairs and competitions, including the amazing International Snow Sculpture Championships each winter. The National Repertory Orchestra and the Breckenridge Music Institute both bring a bit of culture to this high-altitude gem.

Housing includes expensive properties along winding mountain roads and high-end, in-town condominiums.

Population: 5,000 (city proper)

Age 45 or Better: 28%

Median Home Price: $1,000,000

Climate: Summers are short but gorgeous with temperatures in the 70s and 80s. Winters are long with temperatures in the single digits, teens and 20s. On average, the area receives 170 inches of snow and 19 inches of rain per year.

Elevation: 9,600 feet above sea level

At Least One Hospital Accepts Medicare Patients: No, but St. Anthony Summit Medical Center, eight miles away in Frisco, accepts Medicare patients.

At Least One Hospital Accredited by Joint Commission: No, but St. Anthony Summit Medical Center, eight miles away in Frisco, is accredited.

Public Transit: Yes, and it is free.

Crime Rate: Meets the national average.

Public Library: Yes

Political Leanings: Liberal

College Educated: 48%

Is Colorado Considered Tax Friendly for Retirement? Yes

Drawbacks: None

Notes: Tourists are always present. Breckenridge is somewhat isolated.

Dolores, Colorado

Seven thousand feet above sea level in rugged southwestern Colorado, the scenery is breathtaking and the air is thin. It is here in a canyon at the mouth of the Dolores River Valley near the eastern edge of McPhee Reservoir that Dolores makes its home. A ranching community in the 1870s, the little town was later kept alive by the railroad.

With the San Juan National Forest to the east and the Canyon of the Ancients to the west, today Dolores is a hub for outdoor enthusiasts. Residents are a hardy bunch and spend weekends fishing, camping, hiking, biking, rafting and cross-country skiing. Tourists stop in on their way to explore the ancient cliff dwellings in Mesa Verde National Park, 20 miles to the south.

The small downtown is along the river and includes shops, a handful of hotels and motels, the Dolores

River Brewery and the Dolores Food Market, which carries gourmet items.

The Dolores River Festival is a town highlight and features great food and toe tapping music. The farmers' market happens every Wednesday and runs from May to October. Thirty acres of pretty parks with ball fields, trails and river access provide further ways to play outside.

Homes include cabins, chalets, ranch ramblers and Victorians. Three RV parks cater to road warriors and are nestled in the woods.

Trendy, upscale Telluride, home to the Telluride Blues Festival, the Telluride Film Festival, the Telluride Jazz Festival and numerous celebrities, is just an hour and a half away.

Population: 950 (city proper)

Age 45 or Better: 45%

Median Home Price: $380,000

Climate: Summer temperatures are in the 70s and 80s, and winter temperatures are in the single digits and teens. On average, the area receives 18 inches of rain and 68 inches of snow per year.

Elevation: 6,936 feet above sea level

At Least One Hospital Accepts Medicare Patients: No, but Southwest Memorial Hospital in Cortez, eight miles away, accepts Medicare patients.

At Least One Hospital Accredited by Joint Commission: No, but Southwest Memorial Hospital in Cortez, eight miles away, is accredited and is an Adult Level IV trauma center.

Public Transit: No

Crime Rate: Below the national average

Public Library: Yes, and both it and the community center have clubs and classes.

Political Leanings: Very conservative

College Educated: 37%

Is Colorado Considered Tax Friendly for Retirement? Yes

Drawbacks: None

Notes: Dolores has maintained its population within the last decade, but this is a remote place with one two-lane highway in and one two-lane highway out. Winters are long but summers are spectacular. Locals value their privacy.

Glenwood Springs, Colorado

Glenwood Springs is a cozy mountain oasis set amid spectacular, rugged scenery in western Colorado. Outdoor recreation is the hallmark of this area, attracting people who want to spend their days skiing, bicycling, trout fishing, rafting, hiking, golfing, camping or just soaking in the healing waters of the town's famous mineral hot springs.

The atmosphere is part touristy, part collegiate (Colorado Mountain College is here), part Old West, part family-oriented and part mountain funkiness.

Local river rats, college students and older residents mingle with families on vacation, skiers and the occasional cowboy.

The historic Hot Springs Resort Pool, Lodge and Spa, which is Glenwood's primary draw, was built in the 1880s and has the world's largest outdoor hot springs pool. Pool waters stay at 92 degrees Fahrenheit and offer a soothing respite any time of year, even when the snow is falling.

Two rivers, the Colorado River and the Roaring Fork River, converge in town, making fly fishing a favorite pastime. And rafting on the Colorado River through 12-mile-long Glenwood Canyon is a true treat as this stretch of river roars through one of the most scenic spots in all of Colorado.

The Summer of Music Festival, the Glenwood Ave Arts Fest, the Symphony in the Valley and the Glenwood Springs Center for the Arts, to name a few, bring the community together at various times throughout the year.

Dining is adequate, but people seeking more sophisticated cuisine usually travel to nearby Aspen. Here restaurants are chic, expensive and populated with celebrities at adjacent tables.

Home styles include everything from Alpine chalets to condominiums and town homes, many tucked in the woods.

Population: 10,000 (city proper)

Age 45 or Better: 34%

Median Home Price: $665,000

Climate: Summer temperatures are in the 70s, 80s and 90s, and winter temperatures are in the teens, 20s and 30s. On average, the area receives 50 inches of snow and 20 inches of rain per year.

Elevation: 5,761 feet above sea level

At Least One Hospital Accepts Medicare Patients: Yes

At Least One Hospital Accredited by Joint Commission: Yes

Public Transit: Yes

Crime Rate: Meets the national average

Public Library: Yes

Political Leanings: Liberal

College Educated: 35%

Is Colorado Considered Tax Friendly for Retirement? Yes

Drawbacks: Interstate 70 is occasionally congested and can close thanks to snowslides or rockslides. Summer tourist traffic often causes gridlock in Glenwood's downtown/mineral pools section.

Notes: With steep mountains all around, summer days are short (and winter days are even shorter).

Grand Junction, Colorado

Grand Junction sits at the confluence of the Colorado River and the Gunnison River on a high desert plateau west of the Rocky Mountains in rugged western Colorado. It dates from the 1880s and has had a history of cattle ranching, farming and energy exploration. Today, it is home to Mesa University.

An unassuming, quiet place, Grand Junction has a mix of outdoor types, families and retirees in addition to college kids. The downtown area is cozy and cute with outdoor restaurants, art galleries, sculptures, breweries and tree lined streets. The University's lovely Moss Performing Arts Center hosts music and theater productions.

Grand Junction is also known as a mountain biking hub, with riders coming from across the West to test their skills on nearby world class, single lane mountain trails. Residents enjoy hiking and camping in nearby, canyon-laced Colorado National Monument and rafting and fishing along the rivers. The paved Riverfront Trail takes walkers and riders from downtown to the town of Loma, 20 miles away.

Neighborhoods within town are typically suburban and well maintained with bungalows, ranch ramblers and raised ranch ramblers. Downtown has a variety of home styles, including lofts and early-19th century homes.

Outside of town, beautiful properties are nestled in the scrub brush and rocky red terrain. Gorgeous Redlands Mesa is a master planned development that is often called one of the world's most exceptional golf course communities.

Population: 64,000 (city proper)

Age 45 or Better: 40%

Median Home Price: $335,000

Climate: This area has a semi-arid to arid climate. Summer temperatures can reach 100 degrees, and winter temperatures are in the teens, 20s and 30s. On average, the area receives eight inches of rain and 20 inches of snow per year.

Elevation: 4,583 feet above sea level

At Least One Hospital Accepts Medicare Patients: Yes

At Least One Hospital Accredited by Joint Commission: Yes (and one is a Level IV adult trauma center and one is a Level II adult trauma center).

Public Transit: Yes, and the city has a regional airport. Amtrak has a station here with daily service to California and Chicago.

Crime Rate: Meets the national average

Public Library: Yes

Political Leanings: Conservative

College Educated: 39%

Is Colorado Considered Tax Friendly for Retirement? Yes

Drawbacks: The Grand Valley, where Grand Junction resides, is a "bathtub" that traps bad air. Mesa County enacted an ordinance in 2017 that limits open burning has helped, but a large wildfire in California or Utah can still affect ground-level air, making life difficult for people with respiratory issues.

Notes: Grand Junction sits along Interstate 70 but can still feel a little isolated.

Manitou Springs, Colorado

Just to the west of Colorado in south central Colorado, funky, artsy Manitou Springs is a Victorian mountain village nestled in a forested box canyon at the foot of majestic Pikes Peak. It seduces nearly all who come upon it, and in many ways, it feels as though it has been caught in an earlier time.

Manitou appeals to people with a live and let live sensibility. In the 1960s, it was a hippie haven, and today, off the beaten path, it has a mix of families, retirees, old hippies, artists, professionals and others.

Many residences, some restored and others needing a little TLC, date from the late-1800s and early-1900s. Most sit close to one another on narrow, steep streets that radiate from the main road. Dwellings outside of town are mostly expensive chalets and large custom homes and usually come with mountain acreage.

The main road is lined with colorful shops, motor motels and Victorian B&Bs. There are lots of little nooks and crannies with cute restaurants and odd boutiques, making a stroll always a treat. Eight mineral springs bubble up around town, offering water free for the tasting.

Residents have plenty to do, from antique shopping to nearby backcountry camping and fishing. Many of the local attractions, including Cave of the Winds, the Pikes Peak Cog Railway and the Manitou Springs Penny Arcade, are tourist-oriented and are a fun way to spend an afternoon.

Population: 6,000 (city proper)

Age 45 or Better: 42%

Median Home Price: $505,000

Climate: Winter temperatures are in the 20s, 30s and 40s, and summer temperatures are in the 60s, 70s, 80s and 90s. On average, the area receives 19 inches of rain and 54 inches of snow per year.

Elevation: 6,412 feet above sea level

At Least One Hospital Accepts Medicare Patients: No, but University of Colorado Memorial Hospital and Centura Health Penrose St. Francis Hospital are within 10 miles and accept Medicare patients.

At Least One Hospital Accredited by Joint Commission: No, but University of Colorado Memorial Hospital and Centura Health Penrose St. Francis Hospital are within 10 miles and are accredited.

Public Transit: Yes

Crime Rate: Meets the national average

Public Library: Yes

Political Leanings: Split down the middle

College Educated: 40%

Is Colorado Considered Tax Friendly for Retirement?   Yes

Drawbacks: None

Notes: Tourists descend in the summer, clogging the main road and filling up restaurants and shops.

Blue Ridge, Georgia

Surrounded by the Chattahoochee National Forest in the Blue Ridge Mountains of north central Georgia, Blue Ridge started out as a railroad town in 1896. Thanks to its mineral waters, it later became a health resort and at one time boasted five hotels. Today, it is a tourist destination, drawing a lot of Atlanta residents (and others) on weekends.

The cute downtown, particularly Main Street, is noted for its antique stores, brewery, farmers' market, galleries and numerous eateries. The century old train depot, also downtown, is the starting point for daily summer train rides along the scenic railway that runs through the area.

The Arts Center in the renovated Fannin County Courthouse sponsors exhibits and festivals. The community theater produces dramas and hosts live music. Arts in the Park, acoustic music concerts, nightly music jams, ghost walks and historic tours are few of the fun local events. Offering a bit of nostalgia is the Swan Drive-In Theatre, which has been operating since 1955 and is known for its deep-fried Oreos and "fat and sloppy" burgers.

Housing in town is mostly comprised of modest bungalows while residences in the woods range from secluded cabins to large chalets with expansive mountain views. Some of the newer residences are vacation homes.

The neighboring Blue Ridge Lake has miles of shoreline, boat ramps, and a full-service marina. The canoe launch site below the lake's dam allows paddlers access to the Toccoa River.

Population: 1,400 (city proper)

Age 45 or Better: 43%

Median Home Price: $395,000

Climate: Summers temperatures are in the 70s and 80s, and winter temperatures are in the 20s, 30s and 40s. On average, the area receives 65 inches of rain and a dusting of snow each year.

Elevation: 1,725 feet above sea level

At Least One Hospital Accepts Medicare Patients: Yes

At Least One Hospital Accredited by Joint Commission: Yes

Public Transit: No

Crime Rate: Meets the national average

Public Library: Yes, although hours are limited.

Political Leanings: Very conservative

College Educated: 30%

Is Georgia Considered Tax Friendly for Retirement? Yes

Drawbacks: None

Notes: Blue Ridge has been somewhat discovered by baby boomers and is slowly turning into a retirement destination.

Dahlonega, Georgia

In the Appalachian Mountains foothills about 70 miles north of Atlanta, gentle Dahlonega got its start as a boom town during the Georgia Gold Rush of the 1820s. By 1848 most of the gold had been dug out, but Dahlonega managed to survive and eventually became the site of the University of North Georgia, a military college with 6,000 students.

With the development of the Chattahoochee National Forest to the north, Dahlonega also became a popular tourist destination. The cute, historic downtown's galleries, eateries, shops, bookstores along red brick sidewalks are a popular draw. A particular highlight is the Lumpkin County Courthouse, built with gold in its walls and now home to the Gold Museum.

Festivals are many and include the annual Bear on the Square Mountain Festival, held to commemorate the day a bear meandered into town. The Arts and Wine Festival is a juried art competition. The Gold Rush Days brings 200,000 visitors to town for a weekend of gold panning, great food and music.

For theater buffs, local and touring performances take place at the community Holly Theatre. The University's soccer and basketball teams always need new fans. Bird watching, canoeing, hiking, fishing and camping in the serenity of the Appalachians are all close at hand.

The region around Dahlonega is also known for its wine production. Five wineries are just outside of town, and most of them have a tasting room in town.

Population: 7,000 (city proper)

Age 45 or Better: 30%

Median Home Price: $285,000

Climate: Summer temperatures are generally in the 70s, 80s and low 90s, and winter temperatures are in the 30s, 40s and 50s. On average, the area receives 62 inches of rain and a trace of snow each year. Ice storms can happen.

Elevation: 1,450 feet above sea level

At Least One Hospital Accepts Medicare Patients: Yes

At Least One Hospital Accredited by Joint Commission: Yes

Public Transit: Yes, a van service

Crime Rate: Meets the national average

Public Library: Yes

Political Leanings: Conservative

College Educated: 35%

Is Georgia Considered Tax Friendly for Retirement?   Yes

Drawbacks: The poverty rate is above the national average, although much of this is attributed to the student population. Some parts of town have seen better days. The chance of a tornado striking is 92% above the national average.

Notes: Tourists and college students are a constant presence, although there are fewer tourists in the winter and fewer students in the summer.

Hiawassee, Georgia

Nestled on the shores of pretty Lake Chatuge in rolling northern Georgia, Hiawassee is a scenic little town surrounded by the Blue Ridge Mountains and two national forests. The Appalachian Trail, the longest hiking-only footpath in the world, runs next to Hiawassee so hikers often stop into town for supplies and food. In fact, much of Hiawassee's economy depends on tourism and the AP Trail.

Downtown sits along one road and has clothing stores, outfitter shops, eateries, art galleries, antique stores and the like. Insurance agencies, motels, markets and more are on either end of town.

ArtWorks, run by the Mountain Regional Arts and Crafts Guild, hosts workshops. Hiawassee's Georgia Mountain fairgrounds is home to the lovely Fred Hamilton Rhododendron Garden, car shows, a fiddlers' convention and the ever-popular Georgia Mountain Fall Festival. Young Harris College, only 12 minutes away, sponsors concerts and theater performances.

Hiawassee homes are in the woods and are primarily cabins, ranch ramblers and extended ranch ramblers on acreage.

Lake Chatuge is popular with sports fishermen, and opportunities for hiking, camping and mountain biking abound. The 200-slip Boundary Waters Resort and Marina offers boat sales and rentals. Brasstown Bald is the state's highest mountain and the place to take in breathtaking views.

Population: 935 (city proper)

Age 45 or Better: 70%

Median Home Price: $298,000

Climate: Summers temperatures are in the 70s and 80s, and winter temperatures are in the 20s, 30s and 40s. On average, the area receives 56 inches of rain and a dusting of snow each year.

Elevation: 2,025 feet above sea level

At Least One Hospital Accepts Medicare Patients: Yes, Lake Chatuge Regional Hospital

At Least One Hospital Accredited by Joint Commission: No. The nearest accredited hospital is Murphy Medical Center in Murphy, North Carolina, about six miles away.

Public Transit: No

Crime Rate: Below the national average

Public Library: Yes

Political Leanings: Democrats are few and far between.

College Educated: 31%

Is Georgia Considered Tax Friendly for Retirement? Yes

Drawbacks: None

Notes: The area is dotted with family farms, waterfalls and vineyards.

Coeur d'Alene, Idaho

In the beautiful, rugged landscape of northern Idaho's panhandle, picturesque Coeur d'Alene sits along the shores of shimmering Lake Coeur d'Alene, one of the largest freshwater lakes in North America. Steep, pristine mountains, dozens of smaller, high-altitude lakes and seemingly endless forests surround the lake and town.

Cozy, trendy and very relaxed, Coeur has an upscale mountain vibe and an outdoor-oriented lifestyle. Locals enjoy 135 miles of shoreline, with parasailing, water skiing and fishing popular during warm months and ice fishing the favorite pastime during winter months.

Just outside of town limits, hundreds of miles of mountain trails and two downhill ski resorts provide opportunities for snowmobiling, snowshoeing, cross country skiing and downhill skiing.

For golfers, the massive Coeur d'Alene Resort, with its championship golf course and famous floating 14th green, is a delight. It is spread along the lake's eastern shore and has been named by *Golf Digest* as America's most beautiful resort golf course, noting that it is "not just an escape; it is an experience."

Coeur d'Alene, though, is not just about the outdoors. The Coeur d'Alene Symphony performs in the beautiful Salvation Army Kroc Center. The Summer Theatre produces Broadway quality shows each summer, and The Lake City Playhouse mounts several community productions each year.

Shopping and dining options are plentiful, with five-star restaurants, wine shops, bookstores, antique stores, brew pubs and coffee houses dotting the trendy downtown. The Resort Plaza Shops is an upscale, enclosed mall and the site of book signings, fashion shows, concerts and art displays.

The gorgeous Coeur d'Alene public library is a true treat. It is spacious, airy and boasts breathtaking views of Lake Coeur d'Alene. Workshops, lectures, discussion groups and classes are standard fare.

Population: 54,000 (city proper)

Age 45 or Better: 36%

Median Home Price: $535,000

Climate: Summers are glorious with temperatures in the 80s and 90s. Winter temperatures are in the teens, 20s and 30s. The area receives 27 inches of rain and 80 inches each year on average.

Elevation: 2,188 feet above sea level

At Least One Hospital Accepts Medicare Patients: Yes

At Least One Hospital Accredited by Joint Commission: Yes

Public Transit: Yes

Crime Rate: Meets the national average

Public Library: Yes

Political Leanings: Conservative

College Educated: 29%

Is Idaho Considered Tax Friendly for Retirement? Yes

Drawbacks: Wildfires have occurred nearby and may again.

Notes: Tourists descend in the summer, and traffic becomes thick and heavy. Not all long-time locals are happy with the recent gentrification of their old logging town. Located on I-90 and US Highway 95, Coeur d'Alene is accessible, but it is still "way up there" and can feel a little remote.

Sandpoint, Idaho

In Idaho's scenic panhandle, 60 miles south of British Columbia, Sandpoint an outdoor recreation hub. It has won national accolades for its natural beauty and is noted as one of the country's top outdoor towns. *Rand McNally* has called it the most beautiful small town in America.

It is easy to understand why since Sandpoint sits along the northern shore of sparkling Lake Pend Oreille (Pon-da-ray), a 43-mile-long body of water surrounded by blue-hued mountains. Boaters, hikers, fishermen, students (North Idaho College has a small campus here) and snow skiers (Schweitzer Mountain Ski Resort is nearby) all love it here.

Sandpoint has a bit of a resort atmosphere. The trendy downtown boasts restaurants, shops, coffee houses, offices, art galleries and pubs. The brick buildings date from the 19th-century and are in good shape.

And while the great outdoors beckon at every corner, Sandpoint also has a touch of culture. Each August local studios open to the public during the Artist Studio Tour.

For music lovers, the annual Festival at Sandpoint brings a variety of acts to town for 10 days of great tunes and good food. Theatrical performances take place at the Panida Theater, a beautifully renovated 1927 Spanish Mission-style building.

Other events include the annual Winter Carnival and Lost in the 50s, a classic car show. The farmers' market is a popular spot, with fruits, baked goods, cheeses and locally grown huckleberries for sale. Plenty of toe-tapping music is on hand, too.

Population: 9,500 (city proper)

Age 45 or Better: 37%

Median Home Price: $424,000

Climate: Summer temperatures rarely reach 90 degrees and annual rainfall approaches 30 inches. Winters receive up to 80 inches of snow with temperatures in the teens, 20s and 30s.

Elevation: 2,085 feet above sea level

At Least One Hospital Accepts Medicare Patients: Yes

At Least One Hospital Accredited by Joint Commission: Yes

Public Transit: Yes

Crime Rate: Meets the national average

Public Library: Yes

Political Leanings: Conservative

College Educated: 25%

Is Idaho Considered Tax Friendly for Retirement? Yes

Drawbacks: This is a remote region. The nearest interstate highway is an hour away.

Notes: Not all long-time locals are happy with Sandpoint's ongoing gentrification.

Bozeman, Montana

Surrounded by mountains, pretty Bozeman is a friendly city in southwestern Montana. It is also the home of Montana State University and is just 90 minutes from stunning Yellowstone National Park. Interstate 90 runs through the city.

Once just a dusty cow town, today Bozeman is sometimes called Boz Angeles. This is a reference to the number of Californians and other out-of-staters who have made their way here over the last decade.

Bozeman is an outdoor oriented place, but cultural institutions are in good supply, too. They include the Museum of the Rockies, the Montana Arboretum and Gardens and the Pioneer Museum. The busy downtown, situated along wide streets, has a lively nightlife, galleries, a symphony orchestra, an opera association, and theater troupes.

The Emerson Center for the Arts holds classes, concerts and lectures. It also housing galleries, a restaurant, and studios. Locals a enjoy a summer film festival, an arts festival, and a summer music series, too. At least five golf courses have a Bozeman address

The Missouri Headwaters and Hyalite Canyon are among the nearby state parks. Downhill and Nordic ski areas are within easy reach, and the "blue ribbon" trout streams of the Gallatin National Forest are only a few miles away.

Population: 48,000 (city proper)

Age 45 or Better: 40%

Median Home Price: $780,000

Climate: Summer temperatures in the 70s and 80s. Winters bring temperatures in the teens, 20s and 30s. On average, the area receives 18 inches of rain and 84 inches of snow each year.

Elevation: 4,845 feet above sea level

At Least One Hospital Accepts Medicare Patients: Yes

At Least One Hospital Accredited by Joint Commission: Yes

Public Transit: Yes

Crime Rate: Below the national average

Public Library: Yes

Political Leanings: Liberal

College Educated: 56%

Is Montana Considered Tax Friendly for Retirement? Somewhat

Drawbacks: None

Notes: MSU is not known as a party school.

Missoula, Montana

Situated at the foot of the Bitterroot Mountain range in western Montana's Rocky Mountains, Missoula is known as "Garden City" and is home to the University of Montana. Straddling the Clark Fork River, the town sits in a high-altitude valley that was once a glacier lake. National forests and wilderness areas abound, and elk herds graze just outside of town.

The lifestyle is casual, and the ambiance is an interesting combination of Western independence and liberalism. The population is a mix of old school hippies, students, ranchers, affluent urban transplants and smokejumpers (Missoula is a Forest Service base). The city is animal friendly and has won national recognition for being bicycle friendly.

Locals and tourists enjoy camping, hiking, cross country skiing, river rafting, kayaking and golfing (at least seven courses). Fly fishing is particularly popular in these parts, and two nearby sparkling rivers were featured in the 1992 movie *A River Runs Through It.*

UM Grizzlie football, basketball, soccer and cross - country athletic activities ensure that there is always a game to attend. The University's College of Visual and Performing Arts has an extensive calendar.

The Missoula Symphony Orchestra is complemented by the city's alternative music scene. The Missoula Cultural Council supports a wide range of cultural events and groups, including the Downtown Dance Collective and the First Friday Gallery Night.

Montana Shakespeare in the Parks, the Rocky Mountain Ballet Theatre and the Montana Repertory Theatre give residents even more venues for enjoying the arts. There are also plenty of festivals and fairs, from the Garden City Brew Fest to the Montana Festival of the Book.

The downtown is variously described as "trendy" or "pretentious," depending on one's point of view, with restaurants, pubs, shops, coffee houses, bookstores and galleries   The farmers' market, held every summer Saturday and Tuesday, is here, too, and it features fresh produce, baked goods and live music.

For people with a love of learning, UM sponsors the Osher Lifelong Learning Institute, also known as MOLLI. The program is open to anyone age 50 or better and offers a full catalogue of classes.

Population: 76,000 (city proper)

Age 45 or Better: 30%

Median Home Price: $495,000

Climate: Winters are long with temperatures in the teens, 20s and 30s. Skies are gray much of the time, and snowfall reaches 40 inches per year on average. Summers are cool and sunny, with temperatures in the 70s and 80s.   On average, the area receives 15 inches of rain each year.

Elevation: 3,210 feet above sea level

At Least One Hospital Accepts Medicare Patients: Yes

At Least One Hospital Accredited by Joint Commission: Yes

Public Transit: Yes

Crime Rate: Meets the national average

Public Library: Yes

Political Leanings: Liberal

College Educated: 45%

Is Montana Considered Tax Friendly for Retirement?   Somewhat

Drawbacks: None

Notes: Interstate 90 runs through Missoula, but the city is isolated, with open land stretching for miles beyond town limits.

Ruidoso, New Mexico

In the rugged Sierra Blanca Mountains of southern New Mexico and outside of the Ski Apache ski resort, the touristy, laid-back village of Ruidoso makes its home. For much of its history it was a sleepy outpost popular with ski bums, backpackers and cowboys. Today, it is a favorite with vacationers, second homeowners and retirees.

Outdoor recreation is around every corner. The 1.2 million-acre Lincoln National Forest borders part of town, and nearby Bonito Lake is perfect for boating and fishing. Ski Apache is in the neighboring Sierra Blancas and is owned by the Mescalero Apache tribe. Popular with skiers, Ski Apache also draws summer tourists who come to hike and zip line.

Golfers enjoy three public golf courses and two private ones. Four more courses are within 20 miles.

Shops, restaurants, retailers, motels and art galleries, many in adobe-style buildings, line the downtown. Tall pine trees, interspersed among buildings, cast long shadows.

The Spencer Theater for the Performing Arts is a dramatic, world-class facility with eight stories, 500 seats, a waterfall and a crystal lobby. It hosts visiting performances and community presentations throughout the year. The Inn of the Mountain Gods is a hotel, resort and casino on the adjacent Mescalero Apache Reservation

The Golden Aspen Motorcycle Rally draws 35,000 motorcycle enthusiasts every year. The annual Mountain Blues Festival is always packed, and the Ruidoso Art Festival recognized as one of the top juried art shows in the United States.

Population: 8,000 (city proper)

Age 45 or Better: 55%

Median Home Price: $495,000

Climate: Summer temperatures are in the 70s, 80s and occasional 90s. Winter temperatures are in the 30s and 40s. On average, the area receives 35 inches of snow and 20 inches of rain each year.

Elevation: 6,920 feet above sea level

At Least One Hospital Accepts Medicare Patients: Yes

At Least One Hospital Accredited by Joint Commission: Yes

Public Transit: No

Crime Rate: Meets the national average

Public Library: Yes

Political Leanings: Conservative

College Educated: 45%

Is New Mexico Considered Tax Friendly for Retirement? Somewhat

Drawbacks: This area is often in a drought, and some type of water restrictions are usually in place. Wildfires are not unknown. The 2012 Little Bear Fire in nearby Lincoln National Forest was particularly destructive.

Notes: This is a remote area, but U.S. Route 70, which was a major east to west highway before the interstate system arrived, runs through the village.

Asheville, North Carolina

Tucked between the Blue Ridge Mountains and the Smoky Mountains in scenic western North Carolina, Asheville is often hailed as a great place to retire and lands on many "best places to live" lists. It is artsy and funky with a Southern sensibility but also has an emerging resort ambiance.

Tourists flock here year-round, with many coming to see the French Renaissance-style chateau Biltmore Estate that was built by George Vanderbilt II in the late 19th-century. The largest private residence in the world, it has 250 rooms, 8,000 acres and extensive gardens.

The downtown is nicknamed the "Paris of the South" and abounds with comfy cafes, intimate bistros, old fashioned arcades, art galleries, street buskers, antique stores, gothic spires, Art Deco buildings and breweries. In fact, Asheville has more breweries per capita than anywhere else in the U.S. The Grove Arcade is a large, nicely restored marketplace that dates from 1929 and is a great place to buy goods from local merchants.

On the west side of town, the River Arts District is home to artists and musicians, many of whom are renovating old warehouses and giving Asheville much of its creative vibe. Biltmore Village, originally a company town built at the entrance of the Biltmore Estate, is today a charming shopping district.

This beautiful region is rife with outdoor activities, from river rafting and hiking the Appalachian Trail to telemark skiing and driving along the scenic Blue Ridge Parkway. Nearby Shining Rock Wilderness Area and Mount Mitchell, the highest peak east of the Mississippi River, provide a sweeping view of Asheville and the surrounding wilderness.

Population: 92,000 (city proper)

Age 45 or Better: 40%

Median Home Price: $385,000

Climate: Summer temperatures are in the 70s and 80s, and winter temperatures in the 30s and 40s. On average, the area receives 37 inches of rain and 14 inches of snow each year.

Elevation: 2,134 feet above sea level

At Least One Hospital Accepts Medicare Patients: Yes

At Least One Hospital Accredited by Joint Commission: Yes

Public Transit: Yes

Crime Rate: Meets the national average

Public Library: Yes

Political Leanings: Liberal

College Educated: 48%

Is North Carolina Considered Tax Friendly for Retirement? Somewhat

Drawbacks: There are complaints that the city is not particularly clean, and class lines are visible.

Notes: Tourists are wall to wall during the summer months, filling trinket shops, restaurants and roads.

Banner Elk, North Carolina

Banner Elk sits in the Blue Ridge Mountains of northwestern North Carolina, not far from the Tennessee border. It is a popular tourist destination and home to Lees-McRae College, a small private college associated with the Presbyterian Church.

The downtown, which has just one stop light, boasts art galleries, ski shops, boutiques and a craft beer brewery. The dozen or so eateries range from upscale bistros to New York-style delis, and most have a loyal following. The Banner Elk Winery specializes in blueberry and ice wines. It and the Grandfather Vineyard and Winery are just outside of town and open for tastings.

The FORUM Cultural Series, in conjunction with the college, hosts speakers, workshops and more during the summer. Residents also enjoy the Woolly Worm Festival, Art on the Greene, summer concert series in the park and a magical Christmas celebration.

Vacationers and locals alike enjoy skiing at two nearby slopes in the winter, and hiking, ziplining and exploring caverns in the surrounding hills in the summer.

Most homes are nestled in the woods and have a large lot. Mountain views are standard.

Population: 1,500 (city proper)

Age 45 or Better: 25%

Median Home Price: $445,000

Climate: Summer temperatures are in the 70s and 80s, and winter temperatures are in the 20s and 30s. On average, the area receives 55 inches of rain and 42 inches of snow each year.

Elevation: 3,740 feet above sea level

At Least One Hospital Accepts Medicare Patients: No, but Charles A. Cannon, Jr. Memorial Hospital is nine miles away in Linville and accepts Medicare patients.

At Least One Hospital Accredited by Joint Commission: No, but Charles A. Cannon, Jr. Memorial Hospital is nine miles away in Linville and is accredited.

Public Transit: The county has an on-demand van service. Twenty-four hour notice is needed to schedule a ride.

Crime Rate: Meets the national average

Public Library: No

Political Leanings: Conservative

College Educated: 38%

Is North Carolina Considered Tax Friendly for Retirement? Somewhat

Drawbacks: Winter roads are sometimes treacherous.

Notes: This is a rural area - the nearest interstate is 25 miles away. Winter tourism helps keep the feeling of isolation at bay when the snow begins to fall.

Columbus, North Carolina

Tucked in the Blue Ridge Mountains of southwestern North Carolina, about 90 minutes west of Charlotte, Columbus is nice little town in a growing wine and equestrian region. It started out in the mid-1800s and today is the Polk County seat.

With a climate conducive to grape growing, the rolling countryside around Columbus is home to five wineries and more than 20 vineyards. Weekenders from Charlotte and Asheville come for tours and tasting events, giving Columbus a slightly touristy vibe.

The downtown is just four blocks long but lined with red brick buildings that house antique shops, cafes, a brewery and some very good restaurants. It is also home to the county courthouse and two parks. The farmers' market takes place in Courthouse Square or in a church basement year-round.

Museums include the House of Flags and the historical museum. The Tryon International Equestrian Center, packed with all kinds of horse events, is just eight miles down the road.

Population: 1,300 (city proper)

Age 45 or Better: 55%

Median Home Price: $275,000

Climate: Summer temperatures are in the 70s and 80s, and winter temperatures in the 30s and 40s. On average, the area receives 54 inches of rain and four inches of snow each year.

Elevation: 1,105 feet above sea level

At Least One Hospital Accepts Medicare Patients: Yes

At Least One Accredited by Joint Commission: Yes

Public Transit: The county has a call-ahead van service that travels to a regional airport, a Wal-Mart, medical appointments and some other destinations.

Crime Rate: Meets the national average

Public Library: Yes, and everyone seems to love it.

Political Leanings: Conservative

College Educated: 29%

Is North Carolina Considered Tax Friendly for Retirement? Somewhat

Drawbacks: None

Notes: None

Fletcher, North Carolina

Nestled in the Blue Ridge Mountains of scenic western North Carolina, Fletcher is quiet town with a suburban, country vibe. It started out as a railroad stopping point for people traveling between nearby Hendersonville and Asheville.

Residents enjoy a summer music series with concerts in the park. Other events and festivals include an annual chili cook off, a memorial golf tournament and a Christmas tree lighting.

There is no defined downtown area, but Fletcher manages a community park with Cane Creek trails, arboretum gardens and playing fields. A walking trail meanders through Kate's Park next to the library.

Neighborhoods include compact subdivisions with ranch ramblers and peaceful areas with large homes on wooded acreage. Many properties have mountain views.

Population: 8,000 (city proper)

Age 45 or Better: 35%

Median Home Price: $375,000

Climate: Summer temperatures are in the 70s and 80s; winter temperatures are in the 20s and 30s. On average, the area receives 45 inches of rain and six inches of snow each year.

Climate: 2,123 feet above sea level

At Least One Hospital Accepts Medicare Patients: No, but Park Ridge Health is three miles away in Hendersonville and accepts Medicare patients.

At Least One Hospital Accredited by Joint Commission: No, but Park Ridge Health is three miles away in Hendersonville and is accredited.

Public Transit: No

Crime Rate: Below the national average

Public Library: Yes

Political Leanings: Conservative

College Educated: 35%

Is North Carolina Considered Tax Friendly for Retirement? Somewhat

Drawbacks: None

Notes: None

Lake Lure, North Carolina

The resort town of Lake Lure is in western North Carolina's beautiful Blue Ridge Mountains and is nestled around 718-acre Lake Lure, a popular water recreation area. With a mature demographic, this rural oasis has been a favorite retirement spot for years.

Tourists flock here during the summer to enjoy a bounty of outdoor activities. Several movies, including 1987's *Dirty Dancing* and 1992's *The Last of the Mohicans*, were filmed here. One glimpse of the area and it is easy to understand why, as green hills meet crystal blue water to create a breathtaking scene.

The town caters to vacationers with shops, restaurants, campgrounds, hotels and resorts. Otherwise, there is a grocery store, a bank or two, a hardware store and the like.

Residents enjoy a public beach and a public library. Scenic Chimney Rock Park is a nearby mountain recreation area.

Most homes sit in the woods and come in a variety of styles, although many feature cabin or Alpine architecture.

Population: 1,600 (city proper)

Age 45 or Better: 72%

Median Home Price: $350,000

Climate: Summer temperatures are in the 70s, 80s and low-90s. Winter temperatures are in the 20s, 30s and 40s. The area receives 55 inches of rain a year and an occasional dusting of snow.

Elevation: 1,200 feet above sea level

At Least One Hospital Accepts Medicare Patients: No, but Rutherford Hospital is 14 miles away and accepts Medicare patients.

At Least One Hospital Accredited by Joint Commission: No, but Rutherford Hospital is 14 miles away and is accredited.

Public Transit: Yes, the country provides a call-ahead, on-demand van service.

Crime Rate: Below the national average

Public Library: Yes

Political Leanings: Very conservative

College Educated: 46%

Is North Carolina Considered Tax Friendly for Retirement? Somewhat

Drawbacks: Summer tourists come in droves, and amenities are limited.

Notes: The main road in and out of town becomes congested on summer weekends.

Ashland, Oregon

Cozy and picturesque, Ashland is swaddled by the rugged Rogue Valley in southwestern Oregon. Once the stomping grounds of Shasta Native Americans, fur trappers and gold miners, today the city has an artsy mountain vibe and abundant charm. It is also home to the Tony Award-winning Oregon Shakespeare

Festival (OSF), an annual event that runs from February through October.

Southern Oregon University, a four-year liberal arts institution, is here, too. It is this blend of deeply ingrained theater culture, collegiate energy and lush Siskiyou Mountains scenery that creates a rich quality of life, attracting retirees to this "Jewel of the Rogue Valley."

More of a phenomenon than a festival, the Oregon Shakespeare Festival is Ashland's lifeblood. Established in 1935, it is one of the nation's oldest and largest non-profit, professional theater companies, drawing 400,000 attendees and mounting 700 to 800 performances each season. Costumed Shakespearian actors meander about town on a regular basis.

Ashland also has 30 art galleries. Most of these are located within a few blocks of each other downtown where there are specialty boutiques, elegant B&Bs, inviting bookstores and cozy coffee shops.

Top notch restaurants, many locally owned, are in good supply. Residents enjoy the products of numerous local wineries, organic food markets and a food co-op. A couple of shopping centers supply the basics, but there are no large retail or discount stores.

For music lovers, Ashland City Band presents free evening concerts during the summer. The Rogue Valley Symphony has a robust schedule. The Beacon Hills Blues Festival takes place in June.

Downtown's 100-acre Lithia Park brims with flowering plants, sparkling green lawns, duck ponds, rose gardens, sycamore trees and romantic, secluded hideaways. It becomes a tapestry of color in the fall and a quiet place to reflect during the winter.

People come here for the theater culture, but they also come for the outstanding outdoor recreation. The Rogue River offers world-class rafting, fishing and boating. Mount Ashland Ski Area has two dozen runs and 80 miles of trails for cross-country skiers. Emigrant Lake, six miles from town, is popular with boaters and swimmers.

Southern Oregon University sponsors an Osher Lifelong Learning Institute (OLLI) in which retirees can take unlimited classes for a reasonable fee. SOU has more than 2,000 OLLI members.

Population: 23,000 (city proper)

Age 45 or Better: 41%

Median Home Price: $558,000

Climate: January daytime highs are usually in the 40s and 50s, with lows in the 20s and 30s. Summer daytime temperatures are in the 70s, 80s and some 90s, with lows in the 50s. Annual rainfall, which often comes in the form of misty drizzle, averages 20 inches. Snowfall is just seven inches per year, on average.

Elevation: 1,949 feet above sea level

At Least One Hospital Accepts Medicare Patients: Yes

At Least One Hospital Accredited by Joint Commission: No, but it is accredited by DNV Healthcare.

Public Transit: Yes

Crime Rate: Below the national average

Public Library: Yes

Political Leanings: Liberal

College Educated: 60%

Is Oregon Considered Tax Friendly for Retirement? Somewhat

Drawbacks: The earthquake risk is well above the national average. During the last few years, the OSF has had to move some performances indoors because of smoke from nearby wildfires.

Notes: While many residents are well-to-do, Ashland also has a lot of idealistic, creative people without much money. Some long-time locals say that the city has become overly touristy and commercialized. Most residents, though, love their town.

Jacksonville, Oregon

Jacksonville is a nice little town nestled amid lakes, rivers and forests between the Cascade Mountains and the Klamath Mountains in rugged southwestern Oregon. It got its start when gold was discovered in 1851.

The new town boomed until 1925 when the railroad passed it by in favor of neighboring Medford. Jacksonville stopped growing and for years was stuck in time. The result is a well-preserved commercial core with 19th-century Classical Revival, Italianate, Queen Anne and Craftsman style architecture. In fact, the entire town of Jacksonville is a National Historic Landmark.

With its hip but understated charm, the town is popular with tourists who come for the history but also for the annual Britt Music and Arts Festival, a fun concert series that happens each summer and fall. Tasteful wineries, cozy B&Bs, eclectic bookstores, cool coffee houses and upscale retailers add to Jacksonville's appeal. Many residents travel to Medford, seven miles to the east, for extra supplies and services.

Housing is eclectic and includes downtown pioneer properties that have been renovated into beautiful condos as well as new Spanish Colonials on the outskirts of town.

More than 320 acres of surrounding woodlands have walking trails. Gorgeous Crater Lake National Park is 90 minutes to the east.

Population: 3,000 (city proper)

Percentage of Population Age 45 or Better: 57%

Median Home Price: $585,000

Climate: January daytime highs are usually in the 40s and 50s, and lows are in the 20s and 30s. Summer daytime temperatures are in the 70s and 80s, and lows are in the 50s. On average, the area receives 19 inches of rain and seven inches of snow per year.

Elevation: 1,569 feet above sea level

At Least One Hospital Accepts Medicare Patients: Yes

At Least One Hospital Accredited by Joint Commission: No, but Providence Medford Medical

Center is seven miles away in Medford and is accredited.

Public Transit: Yes, provided by Rogue Valley Transportation, and it runs to Medford.

Crime Rate: Well below the national average

Public Library: Yes

Political Leanings: Split down the middle

Is Oregon Considered Tax Friendly for Retirement?   Somewhat

Cons: The earthquake risk is significantly higher than the national average, and this part of the country is no stranger to wildfires. In September of 2020, the Almeda Fire burned southeast of Jacksonville, bringing smoke filled skies and destroying two nearby towns.

Notes: Some long-time locals think Jacksonville has become pretentious and a little too big for its britches.   The Pacific Ocean is three to four hours away by car.

Eagles Mere, Pennsylvania

The little village of Eagles Mere is snuggled around Eagles Mere Lake in the unspoiled Endlesss Mountains of northeastern Pennsylvania and started as a family resort in the 1800s. Today it is a vacation destination and popular with retirees.

Nearly the entire town - 234 buildings - is listed on the National Register of Historic Places, and beautiful Victorian, Queen Anne and Prairie School "cottages" built by the original families still stand. Non-residential historic structures include the Eagles Mere Inn (1887), the Sweet Shop (1885) and at least two Catholic and Episcopal churches.

The lake has a boathouse and a marina with small sailboats. The country club has an 18-hole golf course. Residents (and tourists) enjoy two summer antique shows, a fall arts and craft show and summer theater productions courtesy of the Eagles Mere Friends of the Arts group.

There are several museums, a bookstore, an art gallery, a bank and a handful of restaurants, one of which is in a bed and breakfast and another in the historic Eagles Mere Inn. Most services are provided by the county, and further supplies are found in neighboring villages.

Non-historic homes range from rambling ranches and cabins to modern Colonials.

Population: 120 (city proper)

Age 45 or Better: 60%

Median Home Price: $480,000

Climate: Summers are cool with temperatures in the 70s and 80s. Winter temperatures are in the teens, 20s and 30s. On average, the area receives 45 inches of rain and 68 inches of snow each year.

Elevation: 2,061 feet above sea level

At Least One Hospital Accepts Medicare Patients: No. The closest hospital that accepts Medicare patients is 18 miles away in Towanda. A small medical center is eight miles away in LaPorte.

At Least One Hospital Accredited by Joint Commission: No. The closest accredited hospital is in Towanda, about 18 miles away.

Public Transit: No

Crime Rate: Below the national average

Public Library: No

Political Leanings: Conservative

College Educated: 76%

Is Pennsylvania Considered Tax Friendly for Retirement?   Yes

Drawbacks: The nearest interstate highway is 24 miles away.

Notes: This area is very quiet in the winter. The summer population usually swells to 3,000 people.

Jim Thorpe, Pennsylvania

Known as the "Switzerland of America," beautiful Jim Thorpe is nestled along the Leigh Gorge's Lehigh River in eastern Pennsylvania's scenic Pocono Mountains. It is a cute, touristy little village that seems to enchant just about everyone.

The town started out as Mauch Chunk, a Native American term for "sleeping bear." The name changed in 1953 when the widow of renowned athlete Jim Thorpe convinced the struggling coal hamlet to buy her husband's remains and rename the town in his honor. These days, the legacy of Jim Thorpe draws tourists from around the region, but so does the abundant outdoor recreation. Whitewater rafting is particularly top notch.

And the town's extraordinary Victorian architecture, a compact mix of Gothic Revival, Second Empire, Queen Anne, Richardsonian Romanesque, Shingle and more, creates a wonderfully elegant cityscape.

Shopping is mostly of the specialty type, but there is a general store for basic supplies.

Many in-town homes date from the 1800s, while more contemporary dwellings, including ranch ramblers and cabins, are nestled in the surrounding forested hills.

Population: 4,600 (city proper)

Age 45 or Better: 41%

Median Home Price: $225,000

Climate: Summer temperatures are in the 70s and 80s, and winter temperatures in the teens, 20s and 30s. On average, the area receives 45 inches of rain and 30 inches of snow every year. Autumn is particularly spectacular.

Elevation: 730 feet above sea level

At Least One Hospital Accepts Medicare Patients: No, but Gnaden Huetten Memorial Hospital, about 10 miles away in Lehighton, accepts Medicare patients.

At Least One Hospital Accredited by Joint Commission: No, but Gnaden Huetten Memorial Hospital, about 10 miles away in Lehighton, is accredited.

Crime Rate: Below the national average

Public Library: Yes

Public Transit: Carbon County Community Transit offers door to door rides Monday through Friday. The service requires a reservation and is limited.

Political Leanings: Conservative

College Educated: 28%

Is Pennsylvania Considered Tax Friendly for Retirement? Yes

Drawbacks: Some people say the town is a little insular, and it has lost 2% of its population during the last decade.

Notes: New York City is about two hours away and Philadelphia is about 90 minutes away.

Gatlinburg, Tennessee

Sitting along the border of the Great Smoky Mountains National Park in the scenic rolling hills of East Tennessee, Gatlinburg is hemmed in by tall, forested ridges and started out in the early-1800s as a quiet country holler. When the Park opened in 1934, life began to change as people started arriving from across the nation.

Today Gatlinburg is a busy honky-tonk tourist magnet, attracting hundreds of thousands of vacationers every spring, summer and fall. These folks come for the outstanding opportunities to fish, raft, bicycle, camp and hike, but they also come for Gatlinburg's wall-to-wall shops, boutiques, museums, shows and restaurants.

A zipline, a Ripley's Believe It or Not, a mysterious mansion, several arcades, a passion play, ghost tours, strolling musicians, 20 wedding chapels and much, much more all keep visitors entertained. The

Arts and Crafts loop wanders from the studios of whittlers, painters, potters and quilters to the Arrowmont School of Arts and Crafts, the oldest craft school in Tennessee.

Gatlinburg also hosts a songwriters' festival, a river raft regatta, a craftsmans' fair and more. The nearby Ober Gatlinburg is the only ski area in Tennessee, and it boasts a wildlife encounter area, a skating rink, an aerial slide and a gondola.

Housing stock, much of it nestled in the surrounding hills, includes cabins, chalets and condos.

Population: 3,800 (city proper)

Age 45 or Better: 53%

Median Home Price: $445,000

Climate: Summer temperatures are in the 70s, 80s and 90s, and winter temperatures are in the 20s, 30s and 40s. On average, the area receives 55 inches of rain and seven inches of snow each year.

Elevation: 1,298 feet above sea level

At Least One Hospital Accepts Medicare Patients: No, but Leconte Medical Center is 10 miles away in Sevierville and accepts Medicare patients.

At Least One Hospital Accredited by Joint Commission: No, but Leconte Medical Center is 10 miles away in Sevierville and is accredited.

Public Transit: Yes, an extensive trolley system

Crime Rate: Above the national average

Public Library: Yes

Political Leanings: Conservative

College Educated: 19%

Is Tennessee Considered Tax Friendly for Retirement?   Somewhat

Drawbacks: Tourists overwhelm everything from May through September.

Notes: Gatlinburg suffered a devastating fire in 2016. Nearly 2,500 buildings were destroyed. Since then, though, the town has rebuilt and is back to operating as it was before the fire. Most people love Gatlinburg, but others think it is gaudy and over the top.

Sewanee, Tennessee

Home to the University of the South, cozy Sewanee sits atop the beautiful Cumberland Plateau, part of the Appalachian Mountains in lush south central Tennessee. The university, also named Sewanee, is an Episcopal liberal arts college and the heart and soul of Sewanee.

The college's 13,000-acre campus, known as the "Domain," is covered in lakes, caves and forests. The school hosts frequent public lectures, exhibitions and concerts, including Friday Nights in the Park. Theatre/Sewanee, the production arm of the Department of Theatre and Dance, mounts three to four major productions per year.

Summer on campus brings the annual orchestral music festival and the well-known writers' conference. All readings at the conference are open to the public.

Although downtown Sewanee is tiny, it has a lively collection of dining and shopping establishments. The

Sewanee Golf and Tennis Club has nine holes and is set amid unusual sandstone outcroppings.

Natural Bridge and the Mr. and Mrs. Larry Lee Carter Natural Area both have trails and offer amazing views. The nearby South Cumberland State Park features some of state's best hiking trails.

Neighborhoods are leafy, with everything from ranch ramblers and plantation styles to Cape Cods. The Village on Sewanee Creek is a self-sustaining, eco-friendly community.

Population: 2,600 (city proper)

Age 45 or Better: 22%

Median Home Price: $310,000

Climate: Summer temperatures are in the 80s and 90s, and winter temperatures are in the 30s and 40s. The area receives 60 inches of rain and five inches of snow per year on average.

Elevation: 1,959 feet above sea level

At Least One Hospital Accepts Medicare Patients: Yes

At Least One Accredited by Joint Commission: Yes

Public Transit: No

Crime Rate: Well below the national average

Public Library: Yes

Political Leanings: Conservative

College Educated: 75%

Is Tennessee Considered Tax Friendly for Retirement?   Somewhat

Drawbacks: The tornado risk is 175% higher than the national average.

Notes: The University of the South is not known as a party school, but the parties that do happen are primarily at the frat houses.

Signal Mountain, Tennessee

Walden Ridge is a flat mountain ridge that marks the end of the Appalachian Mountains' Cumberland Plateau in southeastern Tennessee. On top of the ridge sits Signal Mountain, a Chattanooga suburb with a country feeling, good schools and gorgeous views of the Tennessee River and Chattanooga.

A town highlight is the Mountain Opry, which showcases bluegrass music and mountain tunes performed by fiddlers, banjo-pickers and harmonica players every Friday night. The Signal Mountain Playhouse is nestled deep in the forest and has two performances, one indoor and one outdoor, each year.

The weekly farmers' market, which is held in the parking lot of the popular Pruett's grocery, is a hoppin' place and has a good selection of jams, grass-fed beef, produce, dairy products and more.

One of the main draws of living here is the nearby Cumberland Trail. A 196-mile system of remote, scenic hiking trails, it follows the ridges and gorges of the Cumberland Plateau.

Neighborhoods are low density with wooded lots. Homes include ranch ramblers, bungalows, chalets, contemporaries and at least one flying saucer house.

Population: 8,700 (city proper)

Age 45 or Better: 48%

Median Home Price: $460,000

Climate: The area has a mild, humid four-season climate. Summer temperatures reach the upper 80s and low-90s, and winter temperatures are in the 30s, 40s and 50s. The area receives, on average, 57 inches of rain and a dusting of snow per year.

Elevation: 1,710 feet above sea level

At Least One Hospital Accepts Medicare Patients: No, but Chattanooga Healthcare System is in Chattanooga and accepts Medicare patients.

At Least One Hospital Accredited by Joint Commission: No, but Chattanooga Healthcare System is in Chattanooga and is accredited.

Crime Rate: Well below the national average

Public Transit: No

Public Library: Yes

Political Leanings: Conservative

College Educated: 69%

Is Tennessee Considered Tax Friendly for Retirement? Somewhat

Drawbacks: The tornado risk is 128% higher than the national average.

Notes: Many more services are in Chattanooga, which involves a drive down the mountain.

Stowe, Vermont

Tucked between Mt. Mansfield State Forest and CC Putnam State Forest in scenic, wooded northern Vermont, Stowe is cute town best known for skiing. It has a "granola," alpine vibe and takes on a storybook quality during the winter.

The Trapp Family Lodge, the Bolton Nordic Center, and the Stowe Mountain Resort draw tourists from around the country. The town manages parks, a community garden, snowshoe trails, a community center, a recreation path, and an ice arena. Helen Day Art Center, which shares space with the library, offers adult education and special events.

Stowe Performing Arts sponsors a free concert series in the meadow beside the Trapp Family Lodge. The Stowe Theatre Guild has been a theater staple for more than 50 years, and the Spruce Peak Performing Arts Center hosts the region's renowned Tango Music Festival.

Fun restaurants, boutiques, craft breweries, and art galleries line Stowe's very charming, very touristy downtown. The farmers' market is usually a hopping place.

This is an area brimming with hiking and biking trails. The Little River runs through town and empties into the Waterbury Reservoir where locals enjoy camping, boating, and swimming.

Homes include Cape Cods, saltboxes, farmhouses and new condos, most tucked in the forest.

Population: 4,500 (city proper)

Age 45 or Better: 37%

Median Home Price: $585,000

Climate: Summer temperatures are in the 70s and 80s, and winter temperatures are in the single digits and teens. On average, Stowe receives 48 inches of rain and a whopping 148 inches of snow each year.

Climate: 889 feet above sea level

At Least One Hospital Accepts Medicare Patients: No, but Copley Hospital is eight miles away in Morrisville and accepts Medicare patients.

At Least One Hospital Accredited by Joint Commission: No. The nearest accredited hospital is Central Vermont Medical Center, 20 miles away in Barre.

Public Transit: Yes

Crime Rate: Meets the national average

Public Library: Yes

Political Leanings: Very liberal

College Educated: 37%

Is Vermont Considered Tax Friendly for Retirement? No

Drawbacks: This area can feel a little desolate in the winter.

Notes: Stowe has two roads in and out, although Interstate 89 is only about 12 miles away.

Abingdon, Virginia

Surrounded by the Blue Ridge Mountains in rolling western Virginia, Abingdon is the Washington County seat and dates from the mid-1700s. It has a lively arts scene and is proud of its heritage.

Main Street is lined with restored Victorian structures and red brick Federal-style buildings with white-frame windows. The antique shops, music stores, tea parlors and cafes have steady followings.

The William King Museum has five galleries and sponsors artist talks as well as workshops. The Barter Theatre boasts a full season of performances and a long list of famous alumni, including Ernest Borgnine and Gregory Peck.

Abingdon's Arts Depot hosts studios, classes and the Appalachian Center for Poets and Writers. Heartwood is a community gathering place and a social hub for local craftsmen, foodies, and musicians.

The town highlights its heritage with celebrations such as the Crooked Road Music Fest and the Virginia Highlands Festival. Abingdon is the final stop on the Virginia Creeper Trail and at the northern tip of the Overmountain Victory Trail.

Neighborhoods are leafy, and some have red brick sidewalks. Homes are mostly ranch ramblers, raised ranch ramblers, bungalows, plantation-styles and Colonials.

Washington County Park on South Holston Lake includes a boat launch, and the lake permits skiing and fishing. The Mount Rogers National Recreation Area includes the state's highest point, hiking trails, camping, and a fishing lake.

Population: 8,000 (city proper)

Age 45 or Better: 45%

Median Home Price: $210,000

Climate: Summer temperatures are in the 70s 80s and 90s, and winter temperatures are in the 20s and 30s. On average, the area receives 47 inches of rain and 16 inches of snow each year.

Elevation: 2,087 feet above sea level

At Least One Hospital Accepts Medicare Patients: Yes

At Least One Hospital Accredited by Joint Commission: Yes

Public Transit: Yes. District Three Public Transit provides van service in town and transportation to nutrition sites and shopping.

Crime Rate: Below the national average

Public Library: Yes

Political Leanings: Conservative

College Educated: 32%

Is Virginia Considered Tax Friendly for Retirement? Somewhat

Drawbacks: Some people say that Abingdon is a little insular.

Notes: None

Blacksburg, Virginia

In southeastern Virginia's Appalachian Mountains, bucolic Blacksburg sits in the New River Valley and borders the Jefferson National Forest. Lush woodlands and farmland are around every corner.

A classic college town, Blacksburg is also home to Virginia Polytechnic Institute and State University (Virginia Tech). The University is the heart and soul of Blacksburg, and it wields significant influence.

The pleasant downtown has been refurbished with red brick sidewalks, benches and Victorian streetlamps. One hundred sixty or more retailers, eateries and art galleries are open for business. Locals enjoy a good selection of restaurants. The farmers' market does a brisk business.

While Virginia Tech draws mostly engineering students, its School of Performing Arts and the Music Department present dances and concerts throughout the year. The inspiring VT Center for the Arts hosts jazz ensembles, poetry readings and more. Hokie athletics have rabid fans, and the town comes to a standstill during home football games.

Many residents work at VT or at one of the VT Corporate Research Center's numerous high-tech companies.

The city has a lot of student-oriented housing, but there are plenty of quiet residential neighborhoods with everything from beautiful custom homes to simple bungalows.

Population: 45,000 (city proper)

Age 45 or Better: 18%

Median Home Price: $320,000

Climate: Summer temperatures are in the 70s and 80s, and winter temperatures are in the 20s and 30s.   On average, the area receives 40 inches of rain and 23 inches of snow each year.

Elevation: 2,005 feet above sea level

At Least One Hospital Accepts Medicare Patients: Yes

At Least One Hospital Accredited by Joint Commission: Yes

Public Transit: Yes

Crime Rate: Below the national average

Public Library: Yes

Political Leanings: Liberal

College Educated: 73%

Is Virginia Considered Tax Friendly for Retirement?   Somewhat

Drawbacks: Blacksburg has a high poverty rate, but this is due to the large student population.

Notes: Virginia Tech has a strong Greek system and a reputation as a party school, but many of the parties are in the frats and sororities.   The entire town is wired, meaning a wi-fi internet connection can be found anywhere.

Morgantown, West Virginia

At the crossroads of Interstate 79 and Interstate 68 in the beautiful Appalachian Mountains of north central West Virginia, friendly Morgantown sits along the banks of the Monongahela River. It is a secluded place, tucked into wooded rolling hills and is home to West Virginia University.

Morgantown has landed on numerous "best places to live and retire" lists and is an active place. The city's economy and identity are closely tied to WVU, but Morgantown is also a port city that ships large amounts of coal.

The downtown, which borders WVU, has a mix of restored 19th-century structures, modern retailers and restaurants. Suburban neighborhoods are tree-lined and distinct. Parks are many, and two biking and walking trails traverse the city and run along the pretty riverfront.

WVU's Creative Arts Center has a robust theater and dance performance schedule, and WVU football games are all-consuming affairs. In fact, the city, except for pubs and bars, nearly closes down during football games.

WVU also has an OLLI (Osher Lifelong Learning Institute) with classes for people age 50 or better.

About 15 minutes outside of town, beautiful Cheat Lake has marinas, restaurants and more.

Population: 32,000 (city proper)

Age 45 or Better: 25%

Median Home Price: $240,000

Climate: Summer temperatures are in the 80s and 90s, and winter temperatures are in the teens, 20s and 30s. On average, the area receives 15 inches of snow and 40 inches of rain per year.

Elevation: 1,045 feet above sea level

At Least One Hospital Accepts Medicare Patients: Yes

At Least One Hospital Accredited by Joint Commission: Yes

Public Transit: The city is known for its fun, innovative Personal Rapid Transit System (MPRT), an electric "people mover" rail system with 73 pods (mini buses) that have just eight seats each. The pods run on eight miles of track and connect the disjointed WVU campus and downtown.

Crime Rate: Meets the national average

Public Library: Yes

Political Leanings: Liberal

Is West Virginia Considered Tax Friendly for Retirement? Somewhat

Drawbacks: Aside from university and a few pharmaceutical and manufacturing jobs, employment opportunities are mostly low wage.

Notes: WVU is known as one of the top five party schools in the country (*Princeton Review*), often securing the number one spot on that list. Some parts of town are best left to students. Half of the Morgantown's population rides the MPRT every day.

Cody, Wyoming

One of the last places settled in the United States, Cody has a definite "Old West" feeling about it. Named after Buffalo Bill Cody, the "Wild West" showman, it sits in the shadow of northwestern

Wyoming's Big Horn Mountains and is the eastern gateway to Yellowstone National Park. In the summer the nearby peaks shimmer in greens and blues, and in the winter, they sparkle with snow.

With Yellowstone just outside of town, Cody attracts a lot of visitors, primarily during the summer months. The town works hard to cultivate and promote its Western heritage for the benefit of tourists, but it is also the real deal.

Residents are independent-minded and practical. Cowboys and ranchers in Stetsons mingle with vacationers, and cattle auctions attract lively crowds. The "Cody Stampede," one of the largest rodeos in the nation, takes place in early July and brings in ranchers and performers from around the West.

Sheridan Avenue, the town's main drag, is lined with western apparel shops, comfort food restaurants, art galleries, furniture stores and souvenir boutiques. The Irma Hotel, an establishment built by Buffalo Bill for his daughter, is a popular restaurant and bar.

The extraordinary Buffalo Bill Center of the West, an unexpected treat in a town this size, is a gorgeous, world-class facility that houses the Buffalo Bill Museum, the Whitney Western Art Museum and much more. Just down the street, the less lofty but nevertheless interesting Dug Up Gun Museum has more than 800 jammed and rusted pistols displayed in the dirt in which they were found.

Shopping and services meet most needs. There are grocery stores, automobile dealers, discount stores, including Walmart, and the like. Many residents do, however, make regular forays to Billings, Montana (100 miles north) to stock up on supplies.

Outdoor recreation is very much a way of life here, with fishing particularly popular. The many nearby lakes, rivers and streams are loaded with native trout and mackinaw. Many of the lakes sit at high elevations, though, so accessing them is often only possible during summer months.

Wildlife viewing west of town, even before entering Yellowstone National Park, is outstanding. At night, stars blanket the sky and coyotes howl in the distance.

Dwellings with horses, corrals and stables are common throughout the area. Some properties abut national forest land.

Population: 9,800 (city proper)

Age 45 or Better: 41%

Median Home Price: $395,000

Climate: Winters usually bring temperatures in the 20s and 30s with 40 inches of snow (the surrounding peaks receive more). Summer temperatures are in the 70s, 80s and 90s, and annual rainfall is about 10 inches.

Elevation: 5,100 feet above sea level

At Least One Hospital Accepts Medicare Patients: Yes

At Least One Hospital Accredited by Joint Commission: No, but West Park Hospital receives excellent reviews.

Public Transit: No, although there is a summertime trolley with limited runs.

Crime Rate: Below the national average

Public Library: Yes, and it is more than 100 years old.

Political Leanings: Conservative

Is Wyoming Considered Tax Friendly for Retirement?   Yes

Drawbacks: Cody has been transitioning from a working ranch and farm community into a resort destination and not always to the delight of long-time locals. Winters are quiet and can feel isolated.

Notes: The city is remote but does have a small, busy airport with flights to Denver, Salt Lake City and other western destinations.

Thanks for reading!

About the Author

Kris Kelley lives in beautiful Colorado has been finding and reviewing great places to retire since 2006. She is an avid traveler, always looking for that hidden gem of a town, whether it be along an ocean, in a desert or on a mountaintop.

Made in the USA
Monee, IL
04 December 2022

19628826R00046